UNDOING *WHAT HAS YOU* UNDONE

D1316912

UNDOING
WHAT HAS YOU
UNDONE

Beth shares the biblical principles that inspired her novel

BETH MOORE

Tyndale House Publishers, Inc.
Carol Stream, Illinois

Visit Tyndale online at www.tyndale.com.

Visit www.BethMooreNovel.com for bonus material, background, and a discussion guide.

TYNDALE and Tyndale's quill logo are registered trademarks of Tyndale House Publishers, Inc.

Undoing What Has You Undone

Designed by Julie Chen

For information about special discounts for bulk purchases, please contact Tyndale House Publishers at csresponse@tyndale.com or call 1-800-323-9400.

ISBN 978-1-4964-3106-6

Printed in the United States of America

23	22	21	20	19	18	17
7	6	5	4	3	2	1

From time to time the Word of God has inspired my heart with fresh expressions through a poem or vignette. This tender place offers a priceless gift, a moment to stop and feel humanity to our bones, to let ourselves have the moment to feel what we feel, to express it in words and realize the wonder that weaves through it all.

My thoughts had pondered here and there about a longer story. Dare I say, a novel? While I grinned at the wildness of that idea, I didn't foresee the now reality of *The Undoing of Saint Silvanus*. But over time, a story began to take life in my thoughts. These people had real lives, and their hurts entered my hurts, along with their stories, their histories, their challenges, and their victories still to come. They became more than a book, more than a story to me.

Until one day, a few years ago, I just kind of got in a spot. Something had happened that I could not tell. You see, that's the thing. Some of our stories involve other people who really don't want their laundry hung out in front of the church.

If we really knew one another's full stories, we would be slack jawed.

It was one of those times when some things revved up, and when I

⚜
VIDEO CLIP
Watch the video clip
Story Reflects Life at
www.BethMooreBookGroup.com
to hear Beth share how her novel,
The Undoing of Saint Silvanus,
relates to her own life experience.

was muted for a while in one way, good stories start coming out all over the place. Because sometimes you really can't tell *your* story; you need to make one up!

The made-up stories may not be real, but they can still be true. They can sometimes give us a picture of our own lives in ways that a journal entry or a blog post just can't. And so *The Undoing of Saint Silvanus* is my made-up story that explains some very real things that we all deal with every day. It was an outlet for me to try to express something that I want to share with you from the Word. In this novel, a family has been blown apart; Satan wants to dismantle their lives and keep them constantly off balance. And I want you to see this principle in Scripture. I'm very, very committed to my calling to teach, and as long as God will let me, I will write Bible studies and teach Bible studies for the rest of my life. But this story was a grace gift from God, a tremendous journey for me to see this story and this idea set free and to see where it would go. And that is the idea that we're going to study together—the undoing.

WHAT THE ENEMY HAS DONE

I don't know what your family was like. I don't know what you come from. I probably come from something a lot like you do, and that is a mixture of the good, the bad, and the ugly. And a lot of those things balanced out. There was a lot of good . . . but sometimes the ugly is just so ugly. And if you'll let me push a little bit further, it's not only so *ugly*, but the ugly happened so *early* that your whole personality began to develop around all of that ugliness. There's a lot of good going on, but it can't seem to undo the ugly.

Here's what I think. I think there's this thing that goes on among us—a kind of big Christian bluff that everything's just fine, going well, and there are no real problems. But deep down we know there's a disconnect. And we know something has to change.

For many, many years of my young life the whole routine was that we went to church in a mess, in a frenzy of conflict, in all manner of chaos and all sorts of insecurity, and then when we got there we became totally different people when we walked in the door. We played church. We got back in the car and in a moment we switched back into those people.

My freshman year of high school I lived directly across the street from our school. My front door faced the front door of the high school. I would literally open up the door, walk down the front steps to the sidewalk, walk straight across and up the stairs and into that school, **and as I did it, I would become with every step a different person.** And I always wondered to myself, *If the person you're faking that you are is who you really wish you were, is it still hypocrisy?* I know the answer. But there is the wish list: *This* is who I wish *I was.*

What do you do with that? I'll tell you it is a train wreck.

In your life, are there places where, or people with whom, you're tempted to put on an act?

Undoing. You may have heard the word especially in the King James Version of Isaiah 6, where Isaiah looks upon the glory of the Lord and says, "Woe is me! for I am undone; because I am a man of unclean lips, and I dwell in the midst of a people of unclean lips: for mine eyes have seen the KING, the Lord of hosts." *Undone. Undone. Undone.*

It's a word that means to feel cut off, to feel like something—if not your very person—has ceased, perished. It's a word that means to feel destroyed.

To feel destroyed. I love that wording. I think it gets to the meat of it. **To feel cut down.**

STORY TO LIFE

Saint Silvanus Methodist Church is cut down in such a way that people feel it may never recover.

Suspicion taints sorrow like few other poisons. Once it is offered in a silver chalice, full and tipping, most people cannot help but sip. Held on the human tongue long enough, its rancid taste turns sweet. Swallowed, suspicion sinks so deep into the mire of bored and fickle hearts that it resurfaces as fact. It killed Saint Silvanus Methodist Church, and at last, it killed her pastor.

Over the years, several valiant efforts were made toward resuscitating the church. But no matter how promising the man at the pulpit, fate seemed to forbid it. It was not a question of God. If God had ever been there, he had vanished without a trace.

No one remembered who first nicknamed the church Saint Sans, but it stuck like storm shutters to broken windows. Some argued that it was a kindness. They could have called it Ichabod, which means, "The glory has departed."

When things happen, like the things that happened to me, or maybe like the things that happened to you, very often it doesn't just stop with victimization. But then we go on and do all manner of ridiculous things and make all sorts of disastrous relational decisions. And that was me . . . until there began to be through the power of the Word of God this gradual **undoing of what the enemy had done.**

Scripture is clear that, **since the Garden of Eden,** Satan, who appeared as the serpent in Genesis chapter three, **has been attempting to undo what the Lord has done.** Now since he cannot undo the Lord, he goes for the dearest things to your heart. If you're a parent, he would go for your children; or he'd attack your marriage; or your mental well-being; your hope. The enemy would go for anything that was not fixed, anything in flux. Everything—*everything*—is game if it's not in a fixed order that cannot be changed. And that means us.

Genesis 2:1-3 says, "Thus the heavens and the earth were finished, and all the host of them. And on the seventh day God finished his work that he had done, and he rested on the seventh day from all his work that he had done. So God blessed the seventh day and made it holy, because on it God rested from all his work that he had done in creation." That only gets us as far as Genesis 2:3.

Genesis 3:1, just a few verses later, tells us, "Now the serpent was more crafty than any other beast of the field that the LORD God had made." And there he was right in the Garden attempting to undo what God had done in the prize creation of the Creator.

That is the reality. And it isn't good news. But there is good news to be found.

No matter how undone you have been, you are not nearly as undone as the enemy meant you to be. Otherwise, the truth is you would not be sitting here reading this with your remotely sane mind. That's what I hope to prove to you. So as much as the enemy has gotten away with in your life, I want to promise you this: He has not taken that nearly as far as he planned to. Not nearly as far.

That is some good news. That is some very good news.

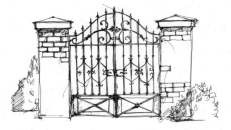

HOW WE ARE UNDONE

What would it look like if the enemy had his full way in a person's life? If the enemy and all the evil that he authors could be in full control, full sway, what would it look like? Because, remember—**he has not done everything he wanted to do**, or we would not be looking into this idea. If he could do everything he wanted to do, what would that look like? What would a person look like if the enemy had complete hold of them?

I'm hoping our eyes spring open if there are some areas in our lives where **the enemy is trying to undo something that God has done in us.**

VIDEO CLIP

Watch the video clip **Why We All Need To Understand "Undoing"** at www.BethMooreBookGroup.com.

I am praying that we would become awake and alert to what the enemy has done. That we would not be ignorant of his devices, and we would do what it takes to cooperate with God to shut down the work of the enemy. And sometimes, if we'll look at the full sway of what it would look like if the enemy got his entire way, maybe then we'd get a little bit of a glimpse of what it would be like to be under demonic oppression.

A trip to the other side

Take a moment, sit back, and really absorb what the Word of God says to us in Mark 5:1-15.

They came to **the other side of the sea**, to the country of the Gerasenes. And when Jesus had stepped out of the boat, immediately there met him out of the tombs a man with an unclean spirit. He **lived among the tombs.** And no one could bind him anymore,

VIDEO CLIP

Watch the video **God Provides Help** at www.BethMooreBookGroup.com to see how Beth shares who inspired her novel's character of David and how this person was a help to her in dark times.

not even with a chain, for he had often been bound with shackles and chains, but he wrenched the chains apart, and he broke the shackles in pieces. **No one had the strength to subdue him.** Night and day among the tombs and on the mountains he was always crying out and **cutting himself with stones.** And when he saw Jesus from afar, he ran and fell down before him. And crying out with a loud voice, he said, "What have you to do with me, Jesus, Son of the Most High God? I adjure you by God, do not torment me." For he was saying to him, "Come out of the man, you unclean spirit!" And Jesus asked him, "What is your name?" He replied, "My name is Legion, for we are many." And he begged him earnestly not to send them out of the country. Now a great herd of pigs was feeding there on the hillside, and they begged him, saying, "Send us to the pigs; let us enter them." So he gave them permission. And the unclean spirits came out and entered the pigs [one of the strangest moments in all of the Gospels: "entered the pigs"]; and the herd, numbering about two thousand, rushed down the steep bank into the sea and drowned in the sea.

The herdsmen fled and told it in the city and in the country. And people came to see what it was that had happened. And they came to Jesus and saw the demon-possessed man, the one who had had the legion, sitting there, clothed and in his right mind, and they were afraid.

The other side. They went to the other side. In this world we're living in we don't have to get in a boat and go to the other side, because the other side has come to us. And sometimes we look in the mirror and see the other side. I wonder if there's anybody reading this right now who has ever looked in your mirror and gone, "Who are you? Who are you! Who are you?" Have you ever become unrecognizable to yourself? Gone through something so hard and become somebody so different, gotten so embittered, so angry, or in just such a stronghold of sin that every now and then you just look in the mirror and think *I'm on the other side*?

I have. I've been there. I know the other side.

STORY TO LIFE

Sometimes what's on the "other side" is obvious, like Rafe's substance abuse or Jade's dead-end search for emotional fulfillment. But it can also look proper and respectable, like Olivia's shuttered heart. But Adella witnessed Olivia's other side in the Great Divulgence. . . .

The most controlled and private person Adella Jane Atwater had ever met was sprawled across the bed half-dressed. The hair she'd kept neatly swept back into a wide barrette every day that Adella had known her was wild and tangled. A swath of it was stuck to the vomit dried on her cheek. Adella had never seen Olivia near a glass of wine, let alone a bottle of bourbon, but one was empty on the floor. She'd obviously pulled out a box of old family photographs because

pictures were strewn around the room, some
of them torn to pieces. A chair was turned over
and the vanity mirror was broken at the upper
right-hand corner, looking like a spiderweb of
glass. Maybe the heel of a shoe, Adella thought
to herself.

And that's where the story begins. It doesn't matter if you
are wearing the cutest shoes in the rain for three hundred
dollars instead of thirty, or if you've got two hundred dollars'
worth of hair color, highlights, lowlights, every kind of lights.
It doesn't matter if you've got your Jesus tattoo, even if you're
a forty-year-old, single virgin. Congratulations. That's a
powerful, powerful thing. But none of that keeps you from
knowing what it's like to come face-to-face with **the other
side** when you're on it. You're on it.

Even if you're a worship leader at your church, someone
well-respected in ministry, you can be encircled by oppression,
but because you've always said that the devil can't do what's
being done to you, you get completely crushed under it. You
might be a Christian counselor who is in scarier shape than
your clients. I'm not throwing shame around here. There's no
condemnation there. I taught Sunday school for twenty-three
years and I'm thinking back on a year of it. You know what? I
just should have sat out for a while and taken myself and my
need and gotten some good counseling. I look back there and
I thank God I wasn't teaching on Periscope. Anybody older like
me think, *What if I had been a young teacher under these condi-
tions and I was getting recorded all the time?* What would we do?

Because there's that margin of growing, and there are seasons when, to be honest, we could all use a little time out, just a little bit of time out.

❧ **What does your "other side" look like?**

❧ **Who knows you well enough to see your other side?**

Jesus has got one huge agenda on the earth. He created the earth so that it could be inhabited by the creation that he would form with his own hands from his own image. The gospel is for people on the other side. I'm going to say it one more time. The gospel is actually for people on the other side.

So, where has Satan gotten to you over and over again? What has driven you to the other side? Because, you see, the enemy is a lot of things, but he's not creative. Only God is the Creator. The enemy is not very creative. He just keeps going for the things that have worked in the past and just keeps working it there. It's a pattern, and we keep repeating it over and over.

And I know this one so well. I know this one by heart because I've lived so much of my life in that pattern. For me, the true breaking free in every sense of the word was broken free and set me free to live life—a life freed from cycling in and out of a deep pit! Maybe it did not look the same from the inside, but it was just as deep and just as muddy and just as hard to get out of.

Where is Satan getting to us over and over again? Because every now and then I just want to say to the body of Christ, "Are any of us really changing at all?" We were meant to be transformed. I don't mean everything is supposed to be happy for us and always great. But I will tell you this, and I believe it with everything in me: Really the gospel is supposed to work. We really are supposed to function well in it, and so we do get to say, "What is awry here?" Do we have guts enough to look in the mirror and just say, **"God, what has gone awry here? Because nothing about this is working. I don't have an iota of joy. I do not feel in the least transformed."**

 Where is Satan getting to you over and over again?

Transformation. Freedom. We'll take a closer look at these in a little bit. But for now, I want us to look a little deeper at what it's like—personally, corporately, globally—when Satan has his full way, because it's right here in this text. Right here as plain as day. In Mark 5, what does it look like?

When Satan has his way, people live among the tombs. One way you know if the enemy is having his way is that you're still clinging to things that are dead. They're over. They're gone. One of the best things that could happen is that something you've been living with for fifteen years is really done now.

STORY TO LIFE

Jillian Slater was clinging to a dream life with her boyfriend, in spite of all the red flags and her own friend's counsel.

At this point, Vince basically owned Jillian. He'd hired her a year ago, and not long after that, they began seeing each other on the side. Those were the good days. He'd talked her into moving in with him about two months ago, but at work, he still acted like he hardly knew her. He said it was to keep things professional.

Jillian hadn't had to deliberate for long when he first suggested she move in. It was so nice to have someone take care of her for a change.

> She'd felt like an adult all her life. Vince was ten
> years older, established and confident, and the
> idea of not being stressed over money was as
> big a lure as the man himself. Her mom under-
> stood how lucky she was. The guy was way out
> of her league. He was gorgeous and loaded
> with cash and could have anyone he wanted.
> He'd chosen her, and she needed him to keep
> choosing her.

I have a friend I love dearly, so there's no disrespect toward this person, but till the day I die, I will remember one conversation as such an example of the mindset we get into. She was in so much angst and discouragement and her entire faith walk was unraveling. She was angry with God. And I simply asked her, "What is it that is keeping you here?" Her pattern was going on and on and on and on. She said, "God told me that man was to be my husband. That we were going to get married." I just scooted up a chair to her and said, "He is now married to someone else and has two children. Now, I don't know what went awry here, but I can tell you something for sure. You're going to have to move on, because there is no way in which you are going to win in the will of God by that man now becoming your husband."

We're waiting to figure out what went wrong, and *then* we'll move on. But there are some things we are not going to understand until we see our Savior face to face and we know as we are known.

I love that wonderful passage out of Psalm 18. I think

about it so often. Where it says with God's help I can leap a wall (Psalm 18:29). Now I think about it because I can just see it. This has happened to me so many times in my life, where I cry, "Why didn't *that* work out? *Why* didn't that work out?" I know what it's like to be devastated over something that just didn't work out.

I don't know how much you know about my longer story. But anybody who was in my Bible studies twenty years ago would know this story well. I had three children instead of two children. We had a little boy, a relative of my husband's, who lived with us from the time he was just barely four years old until he was eleven. And what a complex journey. But I watch a movie like *The Blind Side* and I shout, "Why didn't ours work?" I look at people who have adopted and seem to be living happily ever after. I don't want to take that from them. I don't want anybody to have less of a victory because we didn't get ours. But every now and then I do want to ask, "Hey, what went wrong with ours? We gave it everything we had."

What happened for you? *Lord, what happened with my marriage?* What happened? I've seen that one come full circle all the way around, but I know. I know these kind of questions. And every now and then it's just like God is saying, *"You know what? I'm going to need you to leap over this wall, because that wall's going to stay right here. You're not going to know in this lifetime the explanation for that, but it is time for you to get over this wall. You put your foot right here, Beth, in my hands, and you leap that wall because there's life on the other side."* There's life on the other side, and we've got to get on with it because we're stuck right here at a wall where Satan is having his way.

Write down some of the walls you're facing or old dreams you're clinging to.

People live among tombs when Satan has his way.

I'm going to say something . . . with great compassion. But I'm going to tell you something important. If Satan cannot get you to die *of* your grief, he will do his best to see to it that you die *in* your grief. He doesn't mean for you to get over anything, anything, anything. Just continue to grieve what did not come to pass or grieve that loss, not as one who has hope but as one who is hopeless . . . for the rest of your days. That's what he wants. It can be a relationship way in the past, and we keep trying to breathe life into it, just trying to give a corpse CPR. We're worn out because it's time to move on.

STORY TO LIFE

Reverend Brashear was trapped by the accident that shattered his family.

The malady disabling young Brianna Brashear had left her mother limping as well, though her infirmity was not as clear to the eye. Evelyn Ann doted day and night on her ailing child. She'd taken the pain personally when her daughter's recovery was not all they had hoped and prayed it would be, and she determined to devote the rest of her life to easing the child's burden.

Naturally this left her less available for ministry in the church than many expected. What Mrs. Brashear lacked in congregational servitude, her husband worked tirelessly to compensate for. Reverend Brashear was gregarious, warm, and so unflaggingly energetic that he could wear on the nerves.

Most of the time he seemed unaffected by his helpmate's detachment, but on occasion, a keen observer could see him look toward her with plead-ing eyes, begging her to spring to life and amaze their community with her wit and wisdom. In his rare quiet moments, he couldn't shake the feeling that Evelyn Ann blamed him for Brianna's condition, although for the life of him, he couldn't fathom how. He chose to stay busy, and she chose to let him.

Read the historical story from the novel in its entirety to understand the initial undoing at Saint Silvanus. (Chapters 6, 12, 14, 17, 29, 36, 40, 46, 52, and 57.)

When Satan has his way, people have no voice.
When Satan is having his full sway over an individual, over a group of people, over a community, over a country, you will see over and over again that the people's voices are taken.

Look at what happens in Mark 5:7-9.

And crying out with a loud voice, he said, "What have you
to do with me, Jesus, Son of the Most High God? I adjure
you by God, do not torment me." For [Jesus] was saying to
him, "Come out of the man, you unclean spirit!"
And Jesus asked him, "What is your name?"
He replied, "My name is Legion, for we are many."

Notice with me that the man himself, the true personality,
is not talking here at all. The demon is talking for him. When
Satan has his way over people, their right to speak is taken from
them. They have no voice. Their mouths are shut. And that
is why it is critical that we open our mouths for them. We are
called to speak up for the oppressed. We speak on their behalf
because the mark of the enemy is that he takes away the voice.
He renders it mute. No voice in the government, in a court of
law, in a community, in the home, in a marriages, in all sorts
of relationships. You know the enemy is at work when there can
be no voice, when the mouth is shut.

STORY TO LIFE

*Adella Atwater is one woman who will speak up for
those who can't speak up for themselves.*

"What?" Adella couldn't button her lip to save her life. "Olivia Fontaine, you thank David and Caryn kindly for the offer, but you tell them in no uncertain terms that you will take your own granddaughter to the airport." She wasn't about to let her get away with regressing like that.

"I don't think I can do it. It would be too awkward there on the curb. I don't know what I'd say. We've all got our limitations, Adella. You'd get along better with the rest of humanity if you'd recognize that."

"You drive me crazy, Olivia Fontaine. Stark raving mad. No wonder Mrs. Winsee runs around here in her unders. I've got no problem with limitations, I'll have you know. But I do have a problem with renaming preferences 'limitations.' Here's what you say on the curb, plain and simple: 'I love you, Jillian. I'm glad you are my granddaughter. I don't want to lose touch with you.'"

Satan loves nothing better than to speak for our problems and all our challenges with these words: *Legion. They are many.* He wants you to feel right now like your issues are legion. Maybe you're thinking, *You know what? If I happened to be where I was ten years ago I might really let this lesson land. But it's gone so far now that it's legion. It's legion.* And the enemy shouts over the silence when it seems like heaven is quiet. He shouts to you, "God has abandoned you! He no longer hears you."

But keep in mind that Satan is the father of lies. Instead,

here is some good news. **You have nothing more intimidating to the enemy than your divinely empowered voice.** And you can take that one to the bank. Personally, you have nothing more intimidating. Your gift is not more intimidating. Your talents are not more intimidating. Your education is not more intimidating. Your wealth is not more intimidating. You do not have anything in your life that is more intimidating to the enemy than your mouth, and you need to learn how to use it! Because the devil's two most adamant words to a follower of Jesus are these—"Shut up!" Shut up. He will do anything to shut you up, because if you are in Christ, you have a voice.

There's nothing more powerful than a voice that can utter the words *"Jesus is Lord"* and *"by the power of Jesus' name."* There is nothing more powerful than a voice that can say, *"If God is for us, who can be against us?"* There is nothing—nothing—more powerful than a voice that can say, *"Actually nothing can snatch me out of my Father's hand."* Nothing more powerful than a voice that can say, *"I know whom I believed in, and I am convinced that he is able to protect what has been entrusted to me until that day."* There's nothing more powerful than a voice that can say, *"There is no one like our God. There is no one like Jehovah, and by you I can run against a troop and by my God I can leap over a wall"* (see Romans 8:31; John 10:29; 2 Timothy 1:12; Psalm 18:29).

✠ **What is one way you can use your voice to speak out against Satan?**

Be encouraged. You have a voice and it is powerful in pushing back Satan's full sway. But when that doesn't work, Satan often tries another method.

When Satan has his way, people do self-harm.

Mark 5:5 says, "Night and day among the tombs and on the mountains [the man] was always crying out and cutting himself with stones."

Remember, we are trying to picture if the enemy had his full way in a situation with an individual, with a family, underneath a roof, in a church, in a community, in a country. What might it look like? And here's something we'll see blatantly on the page. Where Satan has his way, people do self-harm.

STORY TO LIFE

Jillian, Rafe, Olivia, Stella . . . practically every major character in the novel faces a measure of self-hatred. For their failings, their unworthiness, their mistakes.

Olivia sat with her jaw fixed, her back rigid, and her hands firmly planted on her knees. Suddenly her head dropped forward and a sound came out of her mouth with a volume that could have curdled blood if not for all the clapping.

Startled, Adella bent over her and asked with ample volume, "Are you alright?" When Adella

put her hand on Olivia's shoulder and felt her
breath break and spasm, the realization hit her
hard. The concrete dam had broken wide open
and so had the heart of a mother of an only son.
Olivia began to wail.

Listen carefully. By no means am I saying that people who
do self-harm are somehow possessed by the enemy. I'm not
even sure I'm prepared to call all of it oppression by the enemy.
Why? Because we've got hearts that are deceitful above all
things, and **one of the strongest things in our human nature
is to be self-destructive and turn on ourselves.**

But I want you to notice. He is cutting himself with stones.
What a picture of the enemy's voice: *Hate yourself. Hate yourself.
Hate yourself. Hate yourself. Hate yourself.* Do you know why the
enemy wants you to hate yourself? Because he hates you. He
hates you because you belong to Jesus and you are loved and
chosen and accepted in the blood. He wants us to turn on ourselves because he is jealous of what we have gained in Christ.

**In what ways does Satan try to get you to hate or harm
yourself?**

Write down a promise from God's Word that you can cling to.

Did you know that according to the Department of Health and Human Services Office on Women's Health, more females intentionally hurt themselves than males? Why is that? What is that? Do we not get hurt enough, so now we must hurt ourselves too? Oh that God would come and deliver us from this stronghold, the shame of self-harm. Because Satan knows that he'll find us most vulnerable when he can isolate us from our true selves, in addition to isolating us from everyone else who might be able to help.

When Satan has his way, people are out of control and out of community.

I want you to notice this, too. Did you notice it says that he lived out among the tombs and he had no longer been able to live in community? To me, this is such a huge part of the saga where Satan has full sway, because **when he has his way, people are out of control and out of community.**

Think about that word *out.* Out. Out. Out. That may be a very tender word to you. It awakens all sorts of terror in you. You have had a safe place to live and someone went out. You have been in a marriage where someone went out. You have been in a relationship where someone went out. You've been employed by someone who just one day went out.

Out. Out. The devil delights in the concept of out.
Out of our minds
out of our homes
out of our community
out of fellowship
out of church
out of friends
out of words
out of a job
out of provision
entirely out of energy
out of answers
out of patience
wholly out of love
out of hope
Out, out, out, out, out, out!

But the gospel tells us exactly the opposite. **We are told over and over again that every single one of us who has placed our faith in the Lord Jesus Christ is *in* and not out, in and not out.** Say it out loud right now, wherever you are:

"I'm in. I am not out."

Because if you are in Christ you are very much in. You are in. And when you are in Christ, nobody—nobody on the planet—can get you out. They can throw you out of a place, but they cannot throw you out of Christ because you are hidden with Christ in God (see Colossians 3:3). And they'd have to come through God, through Christ, to get to you, and that's going to be hard to do. Really, really hard to do.

But Satan doesn't want to just separate us from each other.

The Spirit of God is self-control, but Satan wants us utterly out of control. Mark 5:3 says, "He lived among the tombs. And no one could bind him anymore." No one could bind him anymore. I want you to notice that last word. No one could bind him . . . *anymore*.

You know what the word *anymore* makes me think about? That makes me think they had tried a whole lot of times. When you say, "I can't do it anymore," do you know what I'm going to conclude? I conclude that you have tried to do it a whole lot of times. Is that fair to say? Because if you say, "I cannot do it anymore," I can be certain that you've tried and you've tried and you've tried and you've tried and you have tried.

 Is there something you've tried and tried to subdue that keeps cropping up in your life?

No one had the strength to subdue him.

And so, he was out. Thrown out. Left out. Cast out. Banished to the tombs.

You may know what that's like. I've been both the banished and the banisher. I've had to do it myself in relationships where it is so incredibly unhealthy and so destructive I finally had to say, "I cannot do this any longer. I must draw a line to protect my family here." Maybe you've been trying and trying and trying to subdue somebody. Can you relate?

But nobody has the strength to subdue them.

With man it is impossible. But with God, nothing is impossible (see Matthew 19:26). When Jesus enters in, things start to happen.

UNDOING WHAT IS UNDONE

I've been studying freedom for about fifteen years. It is my life message. It is my testimony. Because I was raised in the church, I've loved Jesus since childhood. So I know what it's like to be raised in that environment and believe it, want it. But at the same time to be in so much bondage that you cannot live out the abundant life filled and empowered by the Spirit. Boy, I know that one. But I'm going to tell you something that I've learned about freedom.

We can help people be delivered by our prayers and by our encouragement. To paraphrase 2 Corinthians, Paul says, "Pray for us that we may be delivered. That God who has delivered and is delivering us will continue to deliver us. And you will help us with your prayers."

STORY TO LIFE

*After facing terrible circumstances, the characters
in the novel share a holy moment of God's peace.*

Olivia fixed her jaw but several tears fought
their way free. She placed her hand on Jillian's.

"Tonight," Jillian said. "Tonight I remembered."

"Christmas is the time for remembering." It
was a strange thing for Vida to say. No proper
time for Merry Christmases. But everyone there
knew the old woman's heart. This night had been
hard for her, too.

Olivia looked at David, who, with elbows on
the table, had dropped his face into his hands.
He didn't appear to be crying. His shoulders were
still. He was just sick at heart, Olivia supposed,
like all of them were.

They all sat silently at the table for what
seemed a good while. Both hands on the mantel
clock had now reached twelve. Olivia opened her
mouth to suggest they blow out the candles and
get to their rooms with the flashlights. The elec-
tricity would surely come back on before morning.

Before she could say a word, David spoke.
"'For I received from the Lord that which I also
delivered to you: that the Lord Jesus on the same
night in which He was betrayed took bread; and
when He had given thanks, He broke it.'"

David reached over to the gold-plated brass
paten and pulled it over in front of him. As the

27

others watched wide-eyed and puzzled, he lowered his chin, whispered the words, "Thank you," and tore the popover into five pieces. He took one piece and handed the plate to Caryn. She stared at him questioningly. When he nodded, she took a piece and passed the plate to Vida. The paten shook slightly in the old woman's hands, but she steadied it with one hand and took her portion with the other. She passed it to Jillian, who knew nothing to do but imitate the others. With one piece of bread remaining on the plate, Jillian passed the paten to Olivia.

David spoke again. "'And the Lord said, "Take, eat; this is My body which is broken for you; do this in remembrance of Me."'"

He put his portion of bread in his mouth. The others hesitated for only the briefest moment before they followed suit.

Once more David spoke. "'In the same manner He also took the cup after supper, saying, "This cup is the new covenant in My blood. This do, as often as you drink it, in remembrance of Me."'"

He reached for the chalice, cupped it in both hands, and held it just below his chin. Unable to look away, Olivia studied David carefully and watched him squeeze his eyes shut. His jaw tightened for several seconds and he pressed his forehead to the lip of the cup. Then he opened his eyes and sipped from it.

When he passed the cup to Caryn, she did not hesitate. She lifted the chalice, took a deep breath, and drank. She held the cup out to Vida, and when she took it in her trembling hands, Caryn wrapped her own hands around the woman's and helped guide it to her mouth. Vida turned toward Jillian, smiled the warmest smile, and extended the cup to her.

Jillian took the gold-plated chalice in both hands. That she carefully and meticulously reenacted David's every move was lost on no one at the table. Jillian squeezed her eyes shut and pressed her forehead to the lip of the cup. After holding it there for several seconds, she opened her eyes and sipped.

At last the chalice passed into Olivia's hands. She stared at it for what felt like a full minute. She lifted her eyes first to David. She shifted her gaze to Caryn. Caryn's eyes met hers and the young woman smiled. Olivia next studied the lined and kind face most familiar to her at the table. Then she looked at the face that most resembled her own, the face of the only one who'd been a stranger to her just months ago.

Lastly Olivia stared at the place at the table Vida had set for an unseen guest. And she took the cup and she drank it.

A year or more ago, I was heading to the airport, at my common stomping ground in Houston. I'd walked into Terminal B, and before the door even shut behind me, a woman stepped in front of me absolutely panicked. She was a young woman, about thirty years old. And she grabbed me and said, "Are you a minister?!" She looked at me. I just said, "Yes." Yes. Yes. I looked around to see if anyone was listening. "Yes." And she grabbed me by the hand and said, "I need prayer!" And she bent her head down and pressed her forehead into my hand. I was just stunned. But I started praying. And about halfway through I started thinking It would help so much if I knew . . . I'm trying to get a word here from God, but I'm still stuck on whether or not I'm a minister. So I leaned into her. She was bent way down. I leaned into her and said, "Can you give me any kind of, like, what . . . what specifically do you want me to pray for?" And she said—I'll never forget it—"My mind! My mind!" Ooh, I so got it. I understood what I needed to ask Jesus for.

 Write the name of someone who needs your prayer support.

If you're somebody who is continuing to cycle into an area of addiction, cycle into an area of defeat over and over again, and you're trying to get some other human to somehow do the trick that is going to set you free, I want you to hear me. They do not have the power to subdue you. They don't have it.

True deliverance in Christ—out of a continual pattern of bondage and sin—takes place one-on-one. Between you and Jesus. I believe strongly in godly counseling. Good counsel can walk us through, talk us through. But your counselor cannot do it for you. Let them be there for you. But there's a work that's got to take place, a work you've got to do with Jesus—with him one-on-one. It's not going to happen any other way because no human being has the strength to subdue us.

Maybe you're mad at somebody you think abandoned you in your struggle. I want to say this as gently to you as I know how: They could not do it anymore. Nobody's having fun with that scenario. They cannot subdue you. They cannot ease your mental anguish, your torment. Only Jesus. It's Jesus. It's Jesus.

And that—*that*—is where a love relationship starts. Talk about falling in love with your hero! When your champion comes and drags you out, there is a romance that begins there that nothing else can match. Nothing.

My husband, Keith, told me a story I'll never forget. He loves to shoot skeet and clay pigeons. In case that's something that's not familiar to you, there's nothing dying there or bleeding. It is a clay disc that's launched up in the air and then he's got to shoot it with a shotgun. He competes in tournaments and really enjoys it. One weekend he was at a tournament with a group of guys, competing against other teams. And one of the guys—a sane person, Keith said; somebody who knew what he was talking about—this guy just looked at the rest of them and said, "I really feel odd about what I'm about to say to y'all, but honestly I could swear to you I just saw a kitten drop out of the sky."

And so they were like, "What?"

He said, "I don't know any other way to tell you. I saw an animal drop out of the sky."

And they said, "How did you see an animal?"

"I saw an animal drop out of the sky."

He was so adamant that the other guys finally went, "You know what? He saw an animal drop out of the sky." So they went looking for the animal, and sure enough, they found a kitten with a broken leg. Needless to say, that kitten was adopted like *that*, because it *fell out of the sky.* If God gives you a kitten, keep the kitten!

Keith said, "I can tell you right now what happened. A hawk got that kitten, and somehow the hawk—probably because the guns were going off and the hawk was going *Waah!*—dropped the kitten."

Listen. There ain't no hawk in the heavenlies that can hold you, when God decides to shoot and set you free. Nothing. Nothing. He can drop kittens out of the sky. Nothing. Nothing. That is deliverance.

✣ **Name something that has a grip on you, where you need Jesus to set you free.**

The enemy would really love to make us all crazy, certifiable nuts, fruitcakes. He would hope to torment us over that situation until we couldn't put three sound thoughts together, because the battlefield—make no mistake—is right up there in our skull. It is time he lost his hold on us, because he does not have this kind of authority.

We're about to turn this story and see what happens when the real authority steps in and begins undoing the undoing.

When Jesus takes authority, Satan loses authority. Where Jesus is invited to exercise authority, Satan's authority is exorcised.

I'm going to say something so common that you might not have even noticed it if I didn't point it out to you. When Jesus takes authority, Satan loses authority. Where Jesus is invited to exercise authority, Satan's authority is exorcised. Do you see it? It's so simple, yet it changes everything.

Our freedom is a matter of authority. I'm passionate about it because I've lived in it. Our freedom is a matter of our being able to submit to the complete authority of God Almighty, who said, "I know the plans I have for you" (Jeremiah 29:11). I know them. I know what I want to do with your life.

There is a gorgeous verse—Joshua 23:14. It almost makes me cry to share it with you. Joshua is echoing what Moses said to him: "And now I am about to go the way of all the earth." So this is Joshua now speaking to the people of Israel. "You know in your hearts and souls, all of you, that not one word has failed of all the good things that the LORD your God promised concerning you. All have come to pass for you; not one of them has failed." Not one of them.

God has a plan. And he will be true to his word. His plan for you is good. It is good. And if we will trust him and if we would believe he is completely for us and never against us, that his authority is not perverse, that God is light and in him is no darkness at all (see 1 John 1:5), then we'll bow down to him and say, "Take over! Take over!"

I look at 2 Corinthians 3:18, and it *doesn't* say, "We all, with unveiled face, beholding the glory of the Lord, are being *tweaked* into the same image from one degree of glory to another." It says we're being *transformed*. Romans 12:2 doesn't say "Do not be conformed to this world, but be *tweaked* by

VIDEO CLIP

Watch the video **Start with God's Redemption in You** at www.BethMooreBookGroup.com to see how Beth encourages you to let God's redemptive light shine through you.

the renewal of your mind, that by testing you may discern what is the will of God, what is good and acceptable and perfect." It doesn't say *tweaked*.

And I want to just throw out to you the thought that we're doing a lot of tweaking, a lot of minor tweaking. But **we're meant to be transformed**. In fact, we are meant to be so transformed that people who have known us start saying, *"Whoa, you are not the same."* We become so changed that we really do give them something to talk about behind our backs. We really are that different. We're not the same people we used to be. The Word of God we're studying makes its way into the marrow of our bones and changes the way we think, and that changes the way we walk.

STORY TO LIFE

Jillian Slater has seen and lived such a mixed-up idea of what relationships and sexuality are all about.

Between the hardships of single parenthood and a couple of broken marriages, Jillian's mom had been treating her like a peer as long as she could remember. On occasion, she came close to treating her like the competition. But Jillian loved her and took up for her ferociously. "She's a free spirit," Jillian always said. "She doesn't live by the rules. To her, they make you common." Jillian's high school friends had been wild about her. Nobody else's mom would let them party like that. Jillian never had the guts to tell her but she wished the surcharge wasn't her partying with them.

Blood was thicker than water, but not always thick enough to blanket every issue. Jade made pretty decent money at an art gallery in the theater district. She lived in a great condo that she'd let one man after another trash for her. She just couldn't stand to be alone. Jade had no idea who she was apart from a man. But Jillian figured no woman did.

You know one reason why we're so sexually messed up? Because we will give God every other part of our lives, but we will not submit that to him and just go, "Lord, you know what? I need some help here. I'm really, really, really unhealthy right there. I seem to be pretty healthy over here, but, Lord, right here somehow sexually I am completely out of control." See, we don't bring that under his authority because we say, "Who wants to talk to God about that?" And so we just leave it messed up, unable to subdue it ourselves.

What undone parts of your life need to come under Jesus' authority?

Authority. He does not force himself on any of us. He has a plan, and he will fulfill it. His Kingdom agenda will be fulfilled, and nobody can stop it. But we can decide not to cooperate with his work of mighty deliverance because we refuse to submit to authority.

Now, for the rest of our lesson, we're going to study what it looks like when Jesus has his way. Notice in Mark 5:15 it says, "And they came to Jesus and saw the demon-possessed man, the one who had had the legion, sitting there, clothed and in his right mind, and they were afraid."

There is nothing that will scare people more than you getting well. **Where Jesus has his way people find the sane place in his presence.**

Where Jesus has his way, people are covered and unashamed. I was looking at the parallel accounts of Matthew, Mark, and Luke. Luke has a version of this story as well, and the wording in Luke strikes me in my bones. In Luke 8:27 it says this: "For a long time he had worn no clothes." For a long time he'd worn no clothes.

STORY TO LIFE

In a Christmas message, Jillian and Olivia hear the truth they need to know about their shame and vulnerability.

Amens and hallelujahs sprang like leaks from pipes bursting with living waters.

"But Jesus didn't come just to live," Pastor Sam continued. "Jesus, the spotless Lamb of God, came to die. By divine plan from before time began, Jesus came to give his perfect life on a cross, bearing all our sin and shame, so that whosoever will—"

Cheers of "Whosoever will!"

"I said, whosoever will!"

Folks looked around at one another, nodding. "He said whosoever will!"

Pastor Sam picked it back up. "So that whosoever, let him come, turning from his own way and believing on Jesus' name, embracing his free gift of grace that no one can earn. . . . Does anybody in the house understand what I'm saying to them tonight?"

Shouts of affirmation all but shook the chandelier.

You remember in the Garden in Genesis 2:25 when Adam and Eve had been unclothed and unashamed? That's the creation narrative. But in the redemption narrative, being unashamed is associated with being covered.

Now, I want you to go with me theologically. I'm not talking about just the physical here. This is not about whether a skirt is too short. I'm talking about theology. And in the creation narrative, it was about being uncovered and unashamed, but after the Fall, God had to cover them with animal skins. And so the whole redemption story, all the way from Genesis 3 to Revelation 22, is all about God covering us. That we're covered and unashamed. We're covered and unashamed. There's a theology of nakedness in the Scriptures. Again, not in anatomy; in theology. And the theology of nakedness is that we are exposed in our folly. You know what that's like.

Has anybody besides me ever just acted a fool in front of a group of people and then you'd have to go back around them again? And just feel like you're standing there in your underwear, because you feel uncovered? But God says, "You know what? Actually, I cover. I cover." And that is where you lose your shame. Nakedness means being open in our shame, exposing our fallenness—be it jealousy, insecurity, whatever it may be.

But here is this guy, and now he's clothed. Been without clothes a really long time, and he's clothed. So where did he get the clothes? I'm just asking. He hadn't worn any clothes in a long, long time. It's not like there's a Nordstrom out in the tombs. I wonder where he got a robe. I just wonder where he got a robe.

Isaiah 61:10: "I will greatly rejoice in the LORD; my soul shall exult in my God, for he has clothed me with the garments of salvation; he has covered me with the robe of righteousness, as a bridegroom decks himself like a priest with a beautiful headdress, and as a bride adorns herself with her jewels."

I was noting in a commentary that this verse depicts exulting that is—and I'm going to quote some of it to you—"extreme and outrageous and demonstrative exhilaration and joy." That term *exult* in Hebrew captures the kind of joy that can be expressed in shouting and dancing and even twirling and spinning.

He has clothed me. In Isaiah 61:10 that word for *clothed* is the same one in the Hebrew, same root word as we find way back in Genesis 3, where it says God clothed Adam and Eve.

We see this idea again in Luke 15:22: "But the Father said to his servants, 'Bring quickly the best robe, and put it on him.'" Robed. Robed.

In Matthew 25:36, Jesus says it again: "I was naked and you clothed me." Not "You took a picture of me and put me on the internet."

 How has Jesus covered you?

You know when God covers us, that does not mean that nobody will ever find out what we've done in secret. We can't know those kinds of things. But here's what we do have. I do think Jesus says, "Be very, very careful about uncovering someone publicly that I have covered." Be very careful. Yes, people are held responsible. Absolutely. There's forgiveness to be sought and solutions and reparations, but he has said that before you publicly unclothe someone, be very careful. I have robed them in my righteousness.

Luke 8:35 in *The Message* says this: "They came to Jesus and found the man from whom the demons had been sent, sitting there at Jesus' feet, wearing decent clothes and making sense." It says these words. I love it: "It was a holy moment."

What Jesus does cannot be undone.

I want you to see something with me as we wrap up. I was reading Isaiah 30 in my time with the Lord one morning, and it stuck out to me so powerfully. Let's circle all the way back to our key term *undoing* and to our premise that Satan's great hope is to undo what God has done.

Read through Isaiah 30:8-18:

And now, go, write it before them on a tablet and inscribe
      it in a book,
that it may be for the time to come
      as a witness forever.
For they were a rebellious people, lying children,
children unwilling to hear the instruction of the LORD;
who say to the seers, "Do not see!" and to the prophets,
      "Do not prophesy to us what is right;
speak to us smooth things, prophesy illusions,
leave the way, turn aside from the path, let us hear
      no more about the Holy One of Israel."

Therefore thus says the Holy One of Israel,
"Because you despise this word and trust in oppression
      and perverseness and rely on them,
therefore this iniquity shall be to you like a breach in a
      high wall, bulging out and about to collapse, whose
      breaking comes suddenly, in an instant;

and its breaking is like that of a potter's vessel that is
    smashed so ruthlessly
that among its fragments not a shard is found with which
    to take fire from the hearth, or to dip up water
    out of the cistern."

Listen to this carefully.
For thus said the Lord GOD, the Holy One of Israel,
"In returning and rest you shall be saved; in quietness
    and in trust shall be your strength."
But you were unwilling, and you said, "No! We will flee
    upon horses"; therefore you shall flee away;
and, "We will ride upon swift steeds"; therefore your
    pursuers shall be swift.
A thousand shall flee at the threat of one;
at the threat of five you shall flee,
till you are left like a flagstaff on the top of a mountain,
    like a signal on a hill.

Therefore the Lord waits to be gracious to you,
    and therefore he exalts himself to show mercy to you.
For the LORD is a God of justice;
    blessed are all those who wait for him.

Listen carefully. Here's what we do: **When we're undone,
we hold on for dear life to what cannot be undone.** I don't
know what has you undone right now. I don't know what may
have you undone in a week or in a month or in six months.
I don't know what has someone in your home completely
undone. I don't know what has your best friend completely

undone. But this I can tell you: **The way to begin undoing what has you undone is to grab on for dear life to that which cannot be undone!** It cannot.

Notice with me that it says in verse 15:

For thus said the Lord GOD, the Holy One of Israel,
"In returning and rest you shall be saved; in quietness
and in trust shall be your strength."

What do you do if you want something done that cannot be undone? Well, if you're God, you just nail it down. You take a hammer and you nail it in place. You drive that nail so far into that wood that what you've put together can't be taken apart. You make sure once and for all that what you've done cannot be undone. But when the devil wants something done that he never wants to be undone, he puts it in a dark hole and rolls a stone in front of it. But the thing of it is when God has a mind to do something, there's no stone big enough to hold him back.

Are you in Christ? Have you trusted him as your personal Savior? I'm not asking, *Have you been raised in the church, have you been raised in the faith? Is your dad a pastor? Is your grandmother an author of all sorts of inspirational books?* I'm asking you: Are you in Christ? Because if you are, that has been nailed down, hammered to a cross, and it is done. It is done and can't be undone. And the enemy tried everything he could to make sure you got stuffed in a dark hole with a stone rolled over it, but that stone was rolled away and Jesus came out of that grave in full triumph and victory. And **everything he has done for you is fully available to you, and once you welcome it, nothing can stop it. Nothing can stop it. The enemy couldn't keep**

Jesus in the dark hole, and he can't keep you there either if you are in Christ.

Our most immediate reflex to the realization that Satan has undone something that God had done in us is to go into a tailspin. It's to get all worked up, write a group email, write a tell-all blog, all of this spinning, just spinning because *we've got to do something!*

You know the first way to undo what the enemy has done? In repentance and rest is your salvation. What is it that cannot be undone? Just stop in Jesus right now and say, "My salvation cannot be undone. Nothing can snatch me out of my Father's hand. You will never cease to love me, because you don't just do love, God; you *are* love. You are love. You will stop loving when you stop being God. Nothing can take you from me, and nothing can take me from you." God's still got that list going, all the good things he has planned for you. Today can be the day to get back to that. Today can be the day when something needs undoing that the enemy has undone.

Sit back and think, *What cannot be undone?* That's where you begin. That's where I began. Grab onto that truth with everything we've got. Right there is where it starts—I know my God is faithful. So recount his faithfulness. Declare it.

⚜ **Name something God has done in you that cannot be undone:**

Write your own declaration of God's unending faithfulness.

I want to show you one last passage. There's the coolest word in Luke 8:38-39. "The man from whom the demons had gone begged that he might stay with him, but Jesus sent him away, saying, 'Return to your home, and declare how much God has done for you.'" One of the commentaires said that it was believed by many in the early church that this was the first act of evangelism—Go back home and tell the people what God has done. "And he went away, proclaiming throughout the whole city how much Jesus had done for him."

You see that word *declare?* In Greek, it's a beautiful, beautiful, beautiful word that looks like this: *diēgéomai, diēgéomai.* And it means "to narrate; to conduct a narration from beginning to end; to tell your narrative." When I wasn't able to publicly tell my own story, I wrote a story that needed to be told. One that I hope you have a chance to read and absorb. But now you must declare your own story.

Oh, you have one. You have a story. I don't know what you've been through, and I don't know how ugly it's been. I know that mine has been terribly, terribly ugly at times. But when you put it together with what your God has done for you that can't be undone, let me tell you, you have a brilliant story.

Write down some key words that describe your story.

 What would you like to see Jesus do in your story?

Some of us are still thinking of our story only in terms of the past—"But, Jesus, ten years ago . . ." That's a beautiful thing. Keep telling it. Because that's an important part of your story. But don't focus so much on the past that you miss what he's doing today. There's something he's doing in you right now, and there's something he's doing in me, and we don't want to miss it. We want to get to the end and say, "Not one word failed" (Joshua 23:14). Not one word.

I want you to read these words out of Revelation 21:1-6. There is a place coming where there is no demoniac. There's just a legion of angels. And the saved and the redeemed gathered around the throne of God.

Then I saw a new heaven and a new earth, for the first heaven and the first earth had passed away, and the sea was no more. And I saw the holy city, new Jerusalem, coming down out of heaven from God, prepared as a bride adorned for her husband.

And I heard a loud voice from the throne saying, "Behold, the dwelling place of God is with man. He will dwell with them, and they will be his people, and God himself will be with them as their God. He will wipe away every tear from their eyes, and death shall be no more, neither shall there be mourning, nor crying, nor pain anymore, for the former things have passed away."

And he who was seated on the throne said, "Behold, I am making all things new." Also he said, "Write this down, for these words are trustworthy and true." And he said to me, "It is done! I am the Alpha and the Omega, the beginning and the end."

Oh, there is a doing that cannot be undone. And you are part of that doing, gathered around that very throne. And this is the day for faith to believe that he who began a good work in you will be faithful to complete it (Philippians 1:6). To believe that everything the enemy has tried to undo will come back upon him, and the snare that he set for you will catch his own ankle, and the pit that he dug for you he will fall into himself. To believe that you

VIDEO CLIP

Watch the wrap-up video **A Blessing to Readers** at www.BethMooreBookGroup.com to hear a clever blessing Beth wrote for readers of her novel, *The Undoing of Saint Silvanus*.

have the right, in the gorgeous and mighty name of Jesus, to make the enemy sorry he ever even knew your name!

Father, in the mighty name of Jesus, set us free this day! Show us, Father, where we have believed lies and where we've fallen for deception. You are faithful and true and cannot do us wrong. You are light, and in you is no darkness at all. In the glorious name and holy name of Jesus, amen.

Saint Silvanus Benediction

May Saint Silvanus still live in us, long past the time the book
  is closed,
To remind us, when we forget again, there's a Savior near
  who knows
That we struggle here with our flaws and fears and forgiving—
  we're not pros.
We've messed up a lot; with friends we've fought and turned
  family into foes.
Jesus comes right in after all our sin and the big fat mess we've
  made and says,
"If you trust me now, I'll show you how to love and hope and
  live by faith."
He can make a household new, like a brand new crew.
And don't tell me that he can't,
For at Saint Silvanus there was God with us,
And he turned sinners into saints.

"From its gritty start to its redemptive finish, Moore's ambitious first novel spotlights her gifts for humanizing the biblical experience and the search for faith."

BOOKLIST

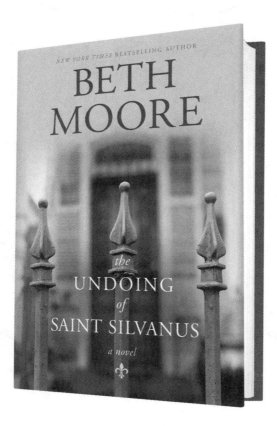

AVAILABLE IN STORES AND ONLINE

Visit BethMooreNovel.com for exclusive content:

- Videos
- Book club packet
- Downloadable resources
- Recipes
- Tour NOLA along with your favorite characters
- Release information
- And more!

Learn to say
good-bye
to insecurity.

So Long, Insecurity Group Experience

Perfect for small groups and Bible studies

NEW YORK TIMES BESTSELLER!

So Long, Insecurity Devotional Journal

Journal with guided questions, Scripture passages, and prayers

The Promise of Security

A portable booklet to carry anywhere

MORE FROM BETH MOORE

BIBLE STUDIES

- *A Woman's Heart: God's Dwelling Place*
- *A Heart Like His*
- *To Live Is Christ*
- *Living Beyond Yourself: Exploring the Fruit of the Spirit*
- *Breaking Free*
- *Jesus, the One and Only*
- *Beloved Disciple*
- *When Godly People Do Ungodly Things*
- *Believing God*
- *The Patriarchs*
- *Daniel*
- *Loving Well*
- *Stepping Up: A Journey Through the Psalms of Ascent*
- *Esther: It's Tough To Be A Woman*
- *James: Mercy Triumphs*
- *Sacred Secrets*
- *Children of the Day*
- *Entrusted*

NONFICTION

- *Audacious*
- *Believing God*
- *So Long, Insecurity*
- *Get Out of That Pit*
- *Feathers From My Nest*
- *When Godly People Do Ungodly Things*
- *My Child My Princess*
- *Whispers of Hope*
- *Praying God's Word*
- *Things Pondered*

DVD TEACHINGS

- *Wising Up Wherever Life Happens*
- *The Inheritance*
- *Here and Now, There and Then*
- *The Law of Love*
- *Breath: The Life of God In Us*
- *The Quest*